AF322942

SKINDIVING

SEÁN

HALDANE

LADYSMITH

Acknowledgments due to *The Shore Review*

Library of Congress Catalogue Card No. 72-88920
ISBN 0-919556-12-4
Québec National Library Legal Deposit 4th quarter 1972
Printed and bound by Les Editions Marquis, Montmagny,
Québec

CONTENTS

THE COAST AND INLAND

(1968)

THE COAST AND INLAND

Our attempts to make love were thwarted :
the clammy weeds and the water clutched us
as we swam naked,
and we slipped apart like fish.
The beach was no better : among the dunes
we found an alcove of thorny bushes
where our flesh was bitten by sand-flies
and sand got between our lips
and between our thighs.

Now I live inland I don't miss beaches,
the sands moving,
the dunes collapsing,
the rocks crumbling,
the waves destroying.
The coast is being eroded —
just as our love was eroded
by such seas of discontent
as could overrun the continent.

CONNEMARA

Fishing where the cold and vicious tide
swept between rocky islands, I dragged in
a monstrous fish,
spiny, luridly scaled, corrupt,
a bull-head. I threw it back.

Later we lived in paradise a week
on the same rocky coast, transformed by sun.
We lay on beaches of pure coral
burning and blinding white. We splashed in the sea
whose cold waves stung our bodies, quickened desire.

Together at evening we climbed through walls,
lifting the stones aside
to find a quiet place among the boulders,
a small patch of green where we could lie.

Then once we drank some poteen.
I wanted, you refused. My jealousy
at your unfaithfulness burned in my brain.
I turned and staggered, struck you to the ground,
then we walked back together in cold shame.

Next day we crossed by boat to Inishmore,
you gay and singing to the other men.
And when we climbed to Dun Aengus fort
I wanted to throw you on the chevaux-de-frise :
each spike of stone went straight up to my heart.
Desperately I pulled you behind the walls
of the fort and begged to make love then,

but you refused, and when we lay on the cliff,
two hundred feet above the emerald sea,
I felt myself vertiginously dragged
close to the edge while you talked happily
and flirted with my friends. I could have died,
but then you brought me home to love again.

That monstrous fish had been my jealousy
which should have lurked for ever in the sea :
it never belonged upon the sunny land.
You knew it, though you did not say,
and wept in silence when I turned away.

WILD HORSES

We, who have lain in fields of heather
naked, defy all changing weather :
the mountains wet, or drying in the sun,
wild horses still in pounding circles run.

THE DIVINE IDIOT

Those dreams when you are hurled about a room,
thudding and bouncing from the concrete walls —
when you look in a clear mirror and see your face
purple, swollen and shining, scarified,
and suddenly the mirror dulls with mist,
then cracks and shatters fragments to the ground.

Those same dreams when you talk with noble birds,
their feathers glowing turquoise and aquamarine,
who fly only to you, so that you can bless them,
sitting upon a throne, raised from your trance
(the fit in which you fell) by a company
of gay yet wistful girls and boys who say,
'You are not sick, we reverence you, friend,
for you have fought the desperate red giant,
hopelessly splintered slats on his rock-hard head,
though he still lives.'
You enter a walled garden with silver fountains
and join to pay court with poets to a naked queen
who lets you touch her thighs.

Those dreams are given life by opposites
condensed in one bright vision. So remember
that if there were no buzzing in your head,
no hideous vibration to make you scream,
you never would be placed upon that throne:
a divine idiot, loved by women,
though somehow differently from other men.

QUI SONO LE MONTAGNE CHE UCCIDONO

When you think of that country, remember
not the ancient squares of the valley town,
nor the paintings in the galleries,
don't even try to make the contrast clear
between north and south — the southern-facing slopes
green with vines, the northern forest-dark,
joined by the summits and the pass we lived in.

Think of the essential things. The crumbling trenches
grass covered long ago, but at the inn
hard-drinking people sing at night
of bursting shells and broken hearts,
the Alpini songs of the First World War.
How sensitive they were, not laughing death off
obscenely, nor sentimental about it,
able to sing of the cold ground,
badly cooked meals and ruined local girls.
Think of their loneliness. Most people here
have a sunless side like the mountains.

'Here it is the mountains that kill'.
When we arrived the rescue team was out
picking up the bodies of a peasant family
whose motor cart had crashed over the edge
of the road in a sudden landslide.

The village was burned by the Germans in the second war
and whole families were shot — the villagers
hid terrorists in the mountains.
Nowadays what crime there is is violent,
often encouraged by the local brandy,
distilled from flower roots.

Remember too the flowers, the sun on the peaks,
the last snow-patches melting near the house
our love was dying in, that mountain spring
when all but we proved adequate to growth.

TWO WORLDS

We sat and talked in a public park
and watched your children playing in the sun,
but our thoughts were of the ancient world of dark
where we had touched and kissed and lain
on a damp river-bank, and at your will
a fish had jumped from the water, silver
under a full moon — fear about to die,
the knife beside me used by you to kill.

THE FUNERAL

Your corpse was carted off to lie in earth.
Part of a tragi-comedy, our tears
were shed — the parson's platitudes in our ears,
the organ, tremulo, playing The Lord Is My Shepherd.
The service, formal prayers for rebirth
said without hope, could not explain the Thing
which made you, once so humorous and stout,
merely a sack of bones for burying.

We are taught to look beyond the flesh-bound self
that feels and eats, and sleeps to rise anew,
but this is the last foul joke — that cheerful you
should cross so huge a gap to show how far
Life is from Afterdeath, and how obscene
whatever lets you rot and does not intervene.

OUT OF SILENCE

Now when I remember you,
the snowflakes in your hair,
the thought is not enough to ease
my gathering despair.

Why should the memory be cold,
though love was still confined ? —
we could not touch, but found some warmth
in closeness of the mind.

We talked about the universe,
the limits of our speech
in telling the effect on us
of what we could not reach —

but felt the rocks hard underfoot,
half covered by the snow.
A universe of death was there.
I knew I had to go.

Next time we meet how can it be
the same between us two ?
Can we not with passion change
the silent winter view ?

Though round that field of drifting snow
run lines of black stone walls,
they cannot spread to prison us
before the darkness falls.

WHY DID I LIE

Why did I lie
when you asked why
my love was not warm still?
I answered so
as not to show
my coldness, lest it kill.

Is it too much
to label such
as lost integrity?
Could it be true
that loving you
I lied more easily?

A PERPETUAL SEASON

Your hair gold, scented with daffodil,
your dress green as a daffodil's stem :
even as winter, outside, chills everything,
your simplicity is a perpetual season
making my blood beat fast as any spring.

HOPE HARD

Though now you walk in this enchanted wood,
and love the flowers dripping in the shade,
you fear the swaying trees of that bright glade
where leaves and grass are spotlit by the sun.

There hounds may chase you, calling for your blood,
you may find death itself is a green mist
rapidly gathering round you, stifling you.

But touch this sheltered myrtle's moistened leaves,
caress tenderly the small flower,
and hope, hope hard. . .

PROSERPINE

I glanced out of my study window
toward the grass and bushes of the valley,
and found her down there.
She sat with her back to me, knitting in the sun,
sometimes tossing her yellow hair.
A small dog squatted beside her.

(Little girl in green, did you know
your presence stirred desire gone dry ?
Was it that which discomforted you
so you rose without turning,
picked your things up and, followed by your dog,
set off along the terrace ?)

The path she has taken through the bushes
leads to a dead end down beside a wall.
There's no way out down there — at least for me.
But possibly for little girls in green
there's some small hidden exit through the scrub.
If I go down there now I still may find her
among the pines and peeling eucalyptus
where periwinkles glimmer in the shade.

MONSERRATE

The grandiose pseudo-Moorish house he built
is empty. Rats and mice have left their droppings
on its cold floors. Last year a forest fire
ravaged the mountain tops and changed the view :
burnt trees stand gallows-like against the sky.

Though thirty soldiers died in the inferno,
the fire was stopped before it reached his garden
(his single work of art) where palms and pines,
Australian freaks and English roses flourish.
The lake is kept clean by workers, tourists come
and breathe the scent of juniper and flowers.
Only the house is dead, the garden lives.

Time helped him make this garden, then he died.
(Perhaps his bones are moss-grown like the trees.)
Others may now find pleasure here and peace,
but they'll die too. This could be Paradise,
but we bring questions with us and our fear :
Is time the friend or enemy of man ?
Must thoughts of death oppress us even here ?

UMA ROSA CAIDA

An ageing, heavy woman shawled in black,
the dim light not kind to her ugly face,
she stood, she sang. Guitars which had been listless
for previous singers, now vibrated loud.
She sang of a fallen rose. 'No, no,' she cried,
'I'll not be jealous though he's left my side —
call me a fallen rose, but I am proud,
I know my own mind, I can well survive —
don't call me jealous, I'm happy and alive.'
Defiantly she sang, her voice so deep
we shivered and held back tears.

Then afterward she smiled and sat to drink
her usual too much whisky with her friend,
the fire of her words there perhaps the same
as when, a rose not fallen, young and slim
she suffered for a better man than him.

MIGRATION

It dropped to freezing point, the sky went gray,
and standing on the long and stony road
we watched a flock of geese upon their way.
Their urgent calling stirred us to the heart,
the movement of continual going south,
though we were travelling northward, here to stay.

THIS DUAL ME

My own the sinister shadow in the snow,
my own the darker self I fear to know,
I come to you in hope you can restore
this dual me to wholeness as before.

THE BRIDEGROOM

The river ice was rearing from its bed
in massive blocks forced upward by the thaw
as we passed by that morning to be married.
Later, out walking on slopes where snow had melted
exposing last year's fallen leaves, you slipped —

'These oak leaves are murder,' kicking them you said,
and I thought of the oak king, bound and crucified,
the drops of my blood trickling down his side.

THE KILLDEERS

Dig up apparently dead beetles
and they'll begin to wake in the warm air,
in resurrection after winter sleep.
It seems that every layer of life is moving,
from deepest worms up to the flocks of geese
passing northward to summer.

But then the plovers flying from the marsh
scream out 'Killdeer, killdeer',
and in our house depression stoops our shoulders.
Our fear of actual death or living death
spoils the season. The glimpse of fertile green
after a shower only makes things worse.
We think with terror of the time
when we'll lie beetle-like beneath the earth
but never rise. There's not enough positive
between us to make us confidently live.

AFFINITY

When we were together
the green and summer showers were fixed,
love seemed eternal.

Then you expelled me to a new world
of desolation and frosted branches
and I alone endured the fall.

Years later now we live
an ocean and a hemisphere apart,
yet in our other world at times I join you:
as I write this I know you think of me,
and time and space are fractured
by our affinity.

THE OCEAN EVERYWHERE

(1970)

THE OCEAN EVERYWHERE

1

When the ocean everywhere moves in us,
dams and breakwaters are swept away
as spring rivers are swept to the sea,
birds swing on threads of gravity
buoyed by the swirling wind,
and the world jerks into oblivion,
our eyes misted as with spray.

2

Clinging to briny moss,
pressing against your island earth
face hard against the wind
I wait for earth to open up a crack
and sea to swallow me.

3

Give yourself up, drift slowly,
currents sweeping down your body
till spent waves eddy in the sand.

Electric charges welling up and over
crests falling in rhythm on the shore,
this is the cosmic pulse, the throb of plasma.

You will not drown — unless your stomach tightens,
your muscles nervously cramp against the bone,
and you lie like a corpse on the waters
till tossed onto cold rocks.

4

The gasping seaman wallows and jerks
among the indifferent waves
of a sea whose storms are futile, climaxless
until it beats on shore — the shore
the seaman seeks, of a warm island
where tides ebb and flow in rhythm
and waves, even, have their end.

There he can rest a while
on a bed of sand where sea is drying,
until he rises and sets out on the surf
to the stirring waters which draw him again
on his long ecstatic journey through the foam.

5

As if the ocean had cast you up
you lay on the beach of our bed,
armpit hollows and crotch
tufted as with crinkly dulse,
tasting of salt :
even land-bound you contained the sea.

6

Outside in streets at dawn
striding through dead leaves,
chilled hands in pockets,

I still carried the scent and musk
of an inside world,
of sea and honey mixed.

7

The rain reminds me of you,
the glistening flowers,
their rising scent,
the dank odour
of the pavement I walk on.

We first embraced
in rain-soaked woods of pine,
first lay together on sodden needles,
first knew each other
in the shadow of cloud-topped mountains.

Remember the release of dammed-up floods
when you cried out you loved me.

8

You taught me to make love slowly,
not violently as before,
to let the feeling swim in us,
not driving stormily, but curving, curling
over and over on a hidden shore,
till earth dissolved in the waves
and our hearts were dislocated by the flow,
the beating everywhere.

PURE CONCENTRATION

Pure concentration is a camera lens
held just above a stream, freezing branches
and the slow ripple of the current's flow
as surely as with ice.

Through concentration you can imagine
just for a moment — while nature perseveres
in its slow motion of change —
your soul in a hole inside your body,
the hollow center of a flame,
a nothing mimicking the outer form.
Pure concentration
is cold as your soul, and dead
as an old photograph.

It's only in a trance of moving thought
that your mind can keep apace
with the warm and turbulently changing earth
as words follow each other like cells
floating in your brain.

Don't fix things, or your brain will cease to move
and you might as well have a stone in your head.
Let your brain live in your body's flow,
the cells, the shifting electric charges.

Let your mind go with your body when it feels
the warm insides of nature. Never forget
your brain itself is flesh.

PAINTINGS BY JEAN-PAUL LEMIEUX
QUEBEC CITY

A monk imprisoned in a white robe,
his neck in a large stiff cowl,
(as if the robe would stand by itself without him)
and people walking in different directions
on a background of infinity.

The theme of the paintings is prison —
of clothes, of solitude.

And the art gallery is next to a prison
which looks like an art gallery
even down to the barred windows.

Both buildings are in the middle of a park,
with a sportsfield and goalposts,
which was once a battlefield.

And inside, in the paintings,
the tall figures face their different ways.

EMBER DAYS

Love took possession slowly as disease,
and blindness came upon me gradually,
as your flaws of complexion and character
faded. Not that I replaced them
with a false image in my mind —
simply they were consumed by my fever.

So when this fall I come home,
light the barbecue, drink beer on the porch
waiting for the heat to reach the grill,
and I miss you — part of a long absence,
not knowing where you are —
I can't say I deceive myself with an ideal.

The blindness of my love for you
is natural and as wholly real
as the invisible flame which moves through charcoal
reducing carefully placed briquettes
to embers and ash. It seems the barbecue
burns under my ribs, in lack of you.

DRUGS

Blue, blue the demon with his flute,
his lower parts, like hers, a tapering wisp,
she, a pink simpering demoness
with rose-tipped breasts. Together they dance.

Avoid blue demons. They will steal your soul,
use your body as a flute for blowing on,
reduce you, though you think you are inspired,
to a smoky freak whose voice is mere hot air.

HANG-UPS

Spring is a messy business here
but the gallows in the garden
rises against leaves or snow or branches
with the same stark look, the same promise of pleasure
to the girl who plays on it thinking it's a swing.

She in fact makes it a gallows:
for all its supple rhythms and strength,
for all her eagerness, the swing
and swing soon chokes her off
in a death of pleasure.

She has too many hang-ups to relax
and drift off on her throbbing seat
to heaven and back. She can't forget the rope.
Choked, she only guesses at
the pulse of swing and spring.

SYMPHONY

Her fingers press the cello's stem
and stroke the stretched sinews
upright between her thighs
as she draws out the tone.

They are all playing the same music,
as lips, hands, instincts move
on membranes, tubes, tensions
yet each is alone.

Her formal dress and the tempo
of the conductor's baton fail to dominate
the suppleness of her body,
the rhythm which is her own,

the intent in her face,
the private progress
to an inner climax :
unlike the people whose minds

wander away from the long melodic sweep,
whose fingers slip nervously
on keys and chords,
who when the music ends

are left fidgety, not serene, who cough
at the pauses between movements,
and whisper — anything
to guard them from the symphony

she makes vibrate across the strings
in waves which go
right to the middle of at least me.

THE SERPENT AND SHE

The serpent of wisdom spoke, and she attended,
yet I could sense her sympathy for me.
My argument she said was nonsense, and yet later
I humbly lay beside her saying I loved her
again and again into her dark hair
and felt her warm flesh tremble at my tongue.

BALLAD

You drank my blood like salty wine
and dined upon my flesh —
you cracked my bones in your hot mouth
and found the marrow fresh.

But though you walk with me inside
no one would ever guess
how much my flesh had entered you
and you would not confess.

At least I know, though lying drained
upon my sheeted bed,
that you still carry where you go
the energy I bled.

And know that though my marrow's sucked
you'll make me whole again,
and find more of the juice and heat
that women like in men.

THE DANCERS

I dreamt the basement of my house caught fire :
I tried stuffing newspapers between the floorboards
but the flames came surging back.

The blaze was put out by two Japanese women dancers
who descended into the basement (which was tiled
like a long bathroom), squatted naked,
and lathered each other with soap beneath a shower.

I followed them there, but the tiles scorched my feet ;
I had to keep running down long corridors
until I came to a bolted iron gate,
and when I started back on cooler floors,
the dancers were gone, I was too late.

A WORD

What time-bombs would I detonate,
what burstings of the heart in its sack?

A word can be the spark
to trigger off explosions in the body.
And if I wrote that word, could we
retreat to frozen dug-outs for defence,
or try to go on as before?

The only way our juices can burst out
is blocked: for us to join,
the earth would have to shrink
to only us, all obligations blown
adrift in space. We could wreck circumstance
and hope to build together on the ruins,
but might be blasted witless by the bang,
our caresses stopping on burnt skin,
our teeth and hair dropping out, and us
lying together
in a charred necropolis.

DISTANCE

At such a distance in years and miles
it's even hard to imagine your body,
and my brain has no antenna for your thoughts,
but I feel a pressure, a dizziness.

My nerves reach to know you again,
I imagine orange-blossoms falling
and clinging in your hair,
while snow is wind-lashed on my cheeks.

Perhaps you open your curly nest
to some lively sub-tropical bird,
red-wattled, rooting lustily,
while I, a northern eagle, stand shivering.

Perhaps the lake you swim in, reflecting pink
from its fluted cliff, shimmers
beneath the sun of a new passion —
or does it shift impatiently against its walls ?

The stream is frozen here,
a few animal tracks on the snow
lead between hairy alders
to the lake and its two-foot ice.

I feel the distance like a spring
coiled against my skin and yours,
expanding between us
to force us further apart.

ZERO NIGHTS

The world is merciless on zero nights.
You know from photographs of the massacred
how human bodies tear,
as the delicate suits of men on the moon could tear,
and leave their corpses brittle on the ground,
flash frozen or scorched to cinders.
You know that everything alive
from the jellyfish to you and your family
is as much in danger on this earth
as men are on the moon.
Feet squeak across the snow in zero weather
then silence returns
and gaunt figures lie glittering on the white.
The rigidness of rock and ice is ours.
Our seismographs record our footsteps —
billions of years behind us and in front,
lifeless, without pulse or mind.

The only milky ways you want to know
are the infant's way, the lover's way,
the milky flow from the breast, the spurt
of milky seed from inside out and in.
The other huge sinister milky way
which girds your sky is part
of zero nights, when you stay indoors,
throw logs on the flames, and know
if fire should fail or burn you up
you'd fall back to the frigid earth.

And yet the quasars pulse, the splitting cell
of life is like a galaxy in birth.
The rays of Northern lights, the sea, the sky,
the water, are your being, and you are theirs.

HAWK'S CRY

I wrote an elegy in a dream
about a master at school, whom I hardly knew.
His nickname was 'Chick', and I remember
his beaked nose, his hands like mottled claws
hooked round the arms of his wheelchair,
his body shrinking with paralysis.

Why should I have to look so far for death ?
Above kingfishers chattering down the stream,
above the crazily zig-zagging snipe
and even above the kingbird,
black-hooded executioner of bugs,
I often hear the throaty call of the hawk.

And yet dream liberates the thought :
too easy to hide beneath flat stones
like a blind and pallid grub,
to lurk in the dark, deny the cruel sky,
keep cool from the beating sun
and hear hawk's cry
only through layers of striated stone.

SKINDIVING

(1972)

SKINDIVING

Two swims in one afternoon — the first in you,
the rhythm slow, the liquids warm, the tide compelling,
a climax of rising cries, descent in spasms . . .

Then in the lake — the waters colder and colder
as I flipper down, odd clicking and gurgling noises,
more a feel than a sound of water in the ears,
a roar at the coldest rhythmless depth,
a turn from rising gravel, weeds and rocks,
to look up at the surface — a burnished mirror,
copper and gold around a liquid sun.

I rise up through layers of color,
clear yellow, clouds of gold-brown motes,
green . . . blue . . . gray . . . then pop out
beside your boat, and climb on clumsily.

A mere damp stain on your bathing suit
reminds me that you hold more lunar rhythms
than any landlocked lake.

MOON-WORLD

We swam in a moon-world — the thousands of bubbles
on our bodies glistened like asteroids,
each murky pit in the lake bottom was a crater,
fish drifted in squadrons like space-ships,
our hair trailed behind us like the tails of comets
in layers of silver light transmuted
by the change of element from air to water,
the cold around us like the cold of space,
the floating weeds phosphorescent as galaxies :
a world where movement was silent and perpetual,
where an invisible wave we stirred might travel
far out of sight to flutter the gills of a fish,
a radiation against the membranes
of the living (who later gently rotted
in the black decay of death in the mud,
or drifted as corpses above the gravel
where eggs had been laid and burst from.)

Experience was pressure : water on eardrums,
the snarl of distant motorboats,
the cold against our shrinking genitals —
a submersion difficult to stay in,
to be sprung out of with a gasp,
a desperate climbing back to normal,
a needed siesta on our matted raft above the deep,
before another plunge, another exploration
of this world opposed to ours
but part of us (in our own bodies the liquids
behind the membrane swelling and pushing,
containing as many creatures as the lake,
stirring up as many nightmares,
as many hidden couplings and dividings of cells —

the liquid also in us, and ourselves
merely the walls of consciousness
between two living flows.)

FOR A FRIEND

At the moment of cutting, the hay
sends up an exhalation of goldenrod and aster
(no wonder the bees attack the mower)
and summer's growth lies on the ground
almost with a gasp.

Too soon sweet turns to sour :
the hay in heaps is pungent in its rotting,
and the apples ripening in the barn
(harvested early to save them from bears)
harbor an ugly spreading brown
under bruised skins.

The images remind me of a friend
who is old, but who keeps
a vigorous sweetness amid the souring
of the mismanaged orchard around him.
His poems are the apples from his tree,
dropped hard at times on frosty ground.
We who have found them over the years
and bitten into the flesh of his thoughts
have found the moment of their falling
stays in their taste.

Bears have attacked his tree time and again,
and the hay above his roots
has been often reaped and thoughtlessly raked away,
yet he has survived, and the generations
of his seedlings will endure.

When at last his tree begins to fall
away from him branch by branch
and the trunk becomes a home for fungus,
I hope he may be granted a dying
as dignified as his life in the orchard corner,
a painless ebbing of the sap.

OVERNIGHT

In bed we raced into the dark
away from the vision of fiddleheads unfurling
green by flowing streams at noon,
to where a single firefly curved
in a muggy night and was gone.

We woke to a steamy dawn : rank ferns
drooping by brackish jungle pools,
and spores invisibly spreading.

FOR A SUCCESSOR OF BRIGID

You took this man and made him new :
he tried to smash his blocks and let out floods,
he struck at dams and dikes
until you made him whole.

What a fine girl, to provide a forge so hot
for the chill-boned fellow,
that he could stretch the giant sinews
which lay hidden under the scrawn,
and forge a hammer to send bearded dwarves
scuttling away from the thundering rivers of the outrush,
and ride in glory on the proud haunches
of you — white mare, smith-goddess,
healer of men.

MIDWINTER RACING

The moment I entered you my heart
began to race toward its pounding finish,
my brain light as a jockey
on the galloping horse of my body
as it surged up and over the leaps
between long rhythmic pacings.

Then I lay perfectly still.
I didn't want to move, but my mind
went wandering : some midwinter spark
from your inner hearth had passed to me,
or had I brought the heat to you,
a radiation from my charging pulse ?

Outside I sawed up wood for an hour,
then waxed my skis and set off
on another race, a fast cross-country run.
My eyes watered against the cold,
my face glowed under my woollen mask
and ice breathed in the lungs was thrown out warm.

At ten below zero the spark was still alive,
and when I came back to you I saw it burned
somewhere deep in you : our casual kiss
was more than a simple greeting,
it was the kiss of two fires lit from the same brand,
though neither knew which way the flame leapt first.

INSIDE

Striated like the inside of a shell
snow lies against our windows, and northern gusts
fill in the paths to our doors.
We're blocked in, but we're not lonely here :
inside, cushions on carpeted floors
are orients of color, and our hirsute jungles,
our earthy cracks and our den-warmth
are far from winter (winter
in our bodies would be death, frozen meat
stored in the ice-box of our house,
limbs hard as statuary, eyes dull as glass,
hair wiry, thin veins ox-blood red).

The smell and feel of living
drift in our rooms, our rugs are warm,
and though our walls are cold to the touch,
their outside surface frosted, we live inside them
full and pulsing as hearts, and steady as motors.
(Our house seems to ride through the snow
sometimes like a ship, with a furnace roar
from our basement engine-room.)

Our house is a shell, our bodies are shells
in a sea of billowing snow whose fish are birds
clinging to kelp-trees in the storm,
whose prowlers of the deep are sea-wolves
in the seaweed-bush. (Inside your bush
it is warm as a wolf's lair, rich in salt-smells,
crannied and pink as coral,
oh glistening mother of the pearls
which form in you.)

I MEANT TO TELL YOU

I meant to tell you about the cracked birches
bent double to the ground,
iced over as if glassed around.

I meant to tell you about the snow
crushed beneath my skis
but then my breath began to freeze.

I meant to tell you ...

LAKE-FISHING

Blue herons rise from their nests
above the pines of their island as we roar by,
and circle up, legs dangling,
a few gaunt mothers the last to leave.
As we veer away we look back down our wake
at them settling again — to eggs addled by chill?
their long throats tight with fear?

After five miles we slow down
and chug back and forth near another island,
our exhaust polluting the water,
and pull in trout: a pulsing weight on the line,
the sight of a yellow flank, a quick splashing
by the boat, then the netting.

I take each heavy fish in both hands
and bash it on the gunwale — blood spatters,
and it twitches in the bow. Each one is 'christened'
with a new drink of rum. We're tipsy
as we head back at dusk, but haul in a big pike
which snaps at my hands as I stun it.

The vee of foam behind us becomes luminous
and the hemlock-covered shores blacken
against an indigo sky. Back at the dock
I can hardly see to gut the fish, but the heads
are phosphorescent as they fall
down through the water.

In the clubhouse, more booze.
I wonder if these fat human bellies under trousers
are fish-white and if I slit them with my knife
what kind of guts would roll out.
No doubt a mass more stinking than pike-offal,
the innards of killers who never kill
(except fish and animals — but it's their own kind
they want to kill).
Watch the looks in their eyes
as they get each other drinks,
watch them skirt around trouble — no pike in the weeds
could be more stealthy. What kind of fight,
I wonder, would they put up on a hook?
No pulsing on the line, surely,
just the long cranking in of a dead weight —
no vicious flapping in the bottom of the boat,
just a whimper and a floundering, rummy puke.

Their women are back home,
glad to be 'fishing widows',
fat on their stale nests, playing bridge.
If they were herons they'd be too torpid
to rise and circle, the motors wouldn't faze them.
And if they were fish? Imagine the dried-up roes,
the grey fat in their sides — but we'd never see them,
they'd never take a bait.

In the fishy jungles of such human minds
there may be tremors among the weeds,
a little friction, the pressures of depth,
vertigo from glimpsing the light above . . .
But quick, take another drink, Men. And Women,
lay out another card. Calm the waters,
calm them now — let the bottom seethe,

you won't feel it. Just let the corpses
accumulate down there — polluted waters
are safe, the twitching will soon be gone,
and in the jungles only the slow descent
of silt upon the stalks of weeds,
and upon the bones
of all those fish that moved.

When your human lake is tamed
no one need know — the waters
may still look blue in the sun.
Only a smell at the edges might betray you,
and the mosquitoes at the dusk of your day,
itching and buzzing from the rot that bred them,
(no more herons on the islands — no fish to feed on).

And frogs whose every slow and labored croak
from the mud anticipates your final breath.

THE WARES OF THE DEAD

It's OK. Open your eyes.
(Half-closed is fore-closed,
a mortgage payable with death.)

Don't flinch. Don't close out the bark and leaves
on the other side of the stream,
don't shrink your brain with half-light.

Let the dead dance, parading their wares,
flashing wigs of straw,
flaunting flesh cool as packed meat.

Don't cut off your own blood,
don't let anger choke your throat,
that throat whose cry
even of bark and leaves
across the stream is real.

Don't deaden your brain with despair,
don't let them calcify it :
gouging it from your skull,
moulding it with lime,
using it as slingshot against each other.

Avoid their slings : let your song
buzz over the battlefield and penetrate
bloody as a bull-roarer
their atrophying heads
and dry their impulse and their skulls.

Their battlefield — clover
stained with blood —
is not the meadow
where you live by a stream
(bark and leaves on the other side)
in another quieter
and deeper world.

APPLE-TIME

The colors of our love are in this orchard —
the purple-pink of our intimate flesh,
the white of our thighs, the barky brown of our hair —
and the smell of our sex in this blossom.
Our mating is the movement of bees
among the flower-tipped spurs of our senses,
we are these trees, trembling in the wind
as our petals are blown and scattered on the grass,
and our skeletal remaining selves
will soon leaf out and contemplate
the hard fruit as it grows,
containing the scent of vanished flowers.

But in our crotches as we sleep at night
the silken cobwebs form, the caterpillars of despair
breed and set forth on journeys, messengers of death
swarming down our limbs, and our leaves
are eaten in our dreams,
and we are left brown and bare and without sap,
the rind of our trunks is bitter with defeat . . .
Until we awake : a new moon,
and we feel our leaves rustle, our fruit hanging
heavy and firm. We are here,
it was only a dream — the brown skeletons —
and we are alive at apple-time.

FATHERS AND SONS

The earth is dry, dry,
insects battle in the dust,
leaves rustle in the heat,
and haze settles on the diminishing river.

I sit reading Turgenev —
poignant as Mozart,
clear as the white wine
in my misted glass.

The book finished, the wine drained,
the thunder breaks, insects lie dead,
are swept away by rain,
into earth which is dark, dark.

LAST THINGS

I am surrounded by last things :
Hemingway's last novel on my table,
Mozart's last opera on the radio,
the last seeds of autumn
on dry stalks outside my window,

and I am about to start on a journey
into unknown country.